T0159036

Letters

to My Teenage

Daughter

We've Got You

GINA ANDREONE
STRAUSS

BALBOA.
PRESS

A DIVISION OF HAY HOUSE

Scripture quotations marked (NLT) are taken from the Holy Bible, New Living Translation, copyright ©1996, 2004, 2007, 2013, 2015 by Tyndale House Foundation. Used by permission of Tyndale House Publishers, Inc., Carol Stream, Illinois 60188. All rights reserved.

THE NET BIBLE*, NEW ENGLISH TRANSLATION COPYRIGHT (c) 1996 BY BIBLICAL STUDIES PRESS, L.L.C. NET Bible* IS A REGISTERED TRADEMARK THE NET BIBLE* LOGO, SERVICE MARK COPYRIGHT (c) 1997 BY BIBLICAL STUDIES PRESS, L.L.C. ALL RIGHTS RESERVED

Balboa Press books may be ordered through booksellers or by contacting:

Balboa Press
A Division of Hay House
1663 Liberty Drive
Bloomington, IN 47403
www.balboapress.com
1 (877) 407-4847

Print information available on the last page.

ISBN: 978-1-5043-9244-0 (sc)
ISBN: 978-1-5043-9246-4 (hc)
ISBN: 978-1-5043-9245-7 (e)

Library of Congress Control Number: 2017918171

Balboa Press rev. date: 01/04/2018

Foreword

Nine years ago, when my daughters were 3 and 4 years old, I received divine inspiration to write a book called "Letters to My Teenage Daughters". I chuckled to myself in that moment because their teenage years seemed so far off. I was proud of our accomplishment of finishing potty training and looking at possible pre-schools, not really thinking of what life would be with teenagers in the house. And yet, that moment came upon us quickly.

As my oldest daughter, Maya, approached her 13th birthday, I wanted to recognize the occasion in a special way. Influenced by a friend who had created a similar scrapbook for her daughter and remembering my earlier inspiration, this book was born.

The idea for a book about womanhood also resonated with me because I have been in the process myself of uncovering what being a woman means to me and after years of shifting through the media imagery and stereotypes of women, exploring the foundation of our patriarchal culture and just plain delving into my life experiences and old beliefs, I felt that I had acquired a bit of wisdom to share.

I believe that it takes a village to raise a child. As it has been for centuries, the elder women in the "village" teach and model womanhood through their stories and their actions. They serve as mentors to these newly emerging youngers. In turn, the girls learn about how to care for themselves and others, participate in community life and most importantly how to navigate life's experiences with honesty, confidence and self-esteem.

With this in mind, I asked a bunch of my dearest family and friends to give their advice and share their stories with Maya. What I received back from them was a collection of insightful, inspiring, humorous, touching, vulnerable and wise letters. I was profoundly moved.

In reading through our anthology, I realized that the wisdom contained in them is wisdom that is timeless and connects us all in community---regardless of our age, skin color, religion, education, monetary wealth, health and life experience. I also realized that the words contained in the letters written by these women who currently live in America in 2017, are truths that have been passed down throughout the ages. It is knowledge that cuts across culture and is found in the sacred teachings of our world's major spiritual beliefs.

At the core is the fundamental truth that we are ONE. It is our imperative to share our stories with our girls---to let them know that they are not alone. We have been there, felt it, done that and are still moving forward on our individual and collective journeys. As our daughters and nieces and granddaughters and students and young friends enter their teenage years, we must remind them of this. We must support each other.

This book is a mixing of our collective wisdom. As you read these letters, please know that they were written for you---substitute your name in the greeting of the letter to feel their power fully. Read one letter a day to savor the words or the whole lot of them in one sitting to let the words flow over you and surround you with inspiration. Whether you are 13, 46, 70 or 101, you can find something to connect to in this book of wisdom. It feels good to have the reminder.

We share our letters with love. Namaste.

Come my dear sisters and spiritual companions;
hug me close in your embrace.
Sri Guru Granth Sahib
Sikhism

Dearest Maya,

In places all over the world, girls are celebrated and honored as they journey from young girls to taking their first steps into womanhood. As you turn 13 today, you are now entering this new part of your journey. I want to honor and celebrate you with the gift of this book.

What I now know, as a woman who has lived 47 years, is that I am a part of an amazing group---the group called women. As women, we are powerful, intelligent, loving, supportive and creative. We have the innate ability to be both incredibly strong and gentle at the same time. We bring forth life and nurture living things with a delicate and firm love. We are beautiful in all our diversity.

This divine femininity that we bring to the world is our greatest gift and now more than ever, our world needs us. This is not to discount or discredit any man, as they are born with a piece of the divine feminine in them too just as we are born with a piece of the divine masculine in us. You have been blessed with many loving and supportive men in your life and for this I am eternally grateful. Your father is a beautiful and kind man who has been my equal partner in our parenting journey and who loves you as much as I do.

This collection of letters is my heart filled gift to you. I have asked women from various walks of my life and yours to offer their stories and their wisdom to you. I include my own story after the others.

In reading this book, I want you to feel, from the bottom of your heart, that YOU ARE LOVED. Loved as you are, simply by being Maya Joy Strauss--no strings attached. I want you to always remember that you have a community of women around you who have been there before and who stand alongside of you rooting you on, whether it be from close by or from afar. Enjoy reading these letters and pull out this book whenever you may need a reminder that "we've got you."

With All My Love,
Mom

Dearest Maya,

I'm so thankful that I get to be a part of your life. You are turning thirteen, a very special turning point for many kids, both boys and girls. You're already such a confident and accomplished young lady with the whole world ready to be molded and experienced by you. You're so much fun and full of joy. I felt very much like you. I was always playful and enjoyed achieving things. However, my story took a turn and I just wanted to share it with you.

Imagine a young girl who at age 13 started high school, ninth grade, as an awkward, out of place, outsider. That was me! I didn't grow up with the rest of the kids at this new school. They all knew each other from elementary and middle school. I just moved from the city to a new neighborhood away from all my friends. I was thrown into a world of teenagers who cared about appearance, designer clothes and popularity while I was still adjusting to no longer being a "tween". I didn't understand cliques and status, what made kids popular and what made them pariahs.

Well, along the way, I came to find that people thought I was a freak because I wasn't quite like they were. I sort of tried to get with the fashion of the time, but I couldn't quite get it right. I was always a bit off and had my own unique way. Boys made fun of me and girls didn't care to associate with me. I thought that being smart was going to help me meet more friends, but instead it made me a target for this one girl who would become my bully. Valerie was her name and she was big and mean! I was small and timid. She made my first year of high school miserable, she along with a boy named Joe.

During this time, I would often get "sick" with stomach aches so that I could stay home. My mom was concerned and would ask if anything was bothering me. I denied that anything was wrong. I felt embarrassed and didn't think my mom would understand what

I was going through. I started to retreat within myself and I became very shy and wanted to disappear.

The thing that I still kept with me was drawing and books. These were my constant companions and comforts. I also had made a few friends. They were kids who let me be me again. Then there was Valerie. She would always bring me back to trying to disappear.

Then hallelujah! It came; it finally came! Summer vacation came and school was over. I was free from the person who made my school life a living hell. I could be myself and play and joke and be a smart-aleck with everyone again. I explored new books and new music.

One day I discovered the one thing that would save my life from the misery and fear that I had experienced in school. There was actually something out there that stimulated my brain and gave me a sense of purpose and belonging. It was raw, misunderstood and not afraid of being different. It was where I belonged as an outsider. It was punk rock! It gave me courage to not be like everyone else. I no longer cared what other people thought of me. It gave me my self-confidence back. It also taught me compassion for others who might not fit in. It gave me strength. Summer vacation was awesome. I wished it would last.

Sadly, September came and school started. It was time for me to really be tested. Oh boy, was I tested! Kids stared. They said mean things. They laughed and pointed. It was pretty harsh, but I kept my chin up. The taunting lessened and my confidence grew. Valerie's comments stopped bothering me and I was no longer afraid of her. I didn't see her that much either. And when I was an 11th grader, I even talked smack back to her which made her friends laugh and stunned her. She was left speechless! It was the last time she ever bothered me! I was free of her for good! I did it. I won. I never let anyone bring me down with their negative words again.

Well Maya, that is my story of being 13. It wasn't a very happy story at first, but I wanted to show you that any kind of teenage obstacle can be overcome and solved. There is always going to be help. There will always be a way out of what seems like it might be forever. Whether you discover the solution yourself or find help from others, teen trials and tribulations are only temporary. Being a teenager can sometimes be hard. I'm sure for you it will be much easier because you have such an awesome support system---your mom, your dad, your friends, your peers, your cousins, your uncles and aunts (like me). If you ever have a time of need, just remember to talk to someone which is something I wish I knew back then.

Always keep your joyfulness, always keep your creativity, and never be afraid to share your voice. I'm proud of the person you're growing into and can't wait to see what else you have in store for the future!

Love,
Aunt Judy

To the Mayans, the jaguar represents the spirit of the feminine. She carries on her back the universe and is fearless, swift, gentle, fierce, smart and beautiful. Grandmother Flordemayo, Central America and New Mexico *Grandmothers Counsel the World*

Dear Maya,

Believe in yourself. Trust your inner voice.

The coming years will be confusing with lots of advice, peer pressure and noise. Try to find yourself in that chaos and believe and trust in you. Try to make decisions based on your own instincts, feelings and knowledge. Know that you will make mistakes and have great successes and that you will learn from both.

Be kind,

be thoughtful,

be gracious,

and most of all…....be confident.

Love,
Ms. Dana

Authenticity is not something we have or don't have. It's a practice---a conscious choice of how we want to life. Authenticity is a collection of choices that we have to make everyday. It's about the choice to show up and be real. The choice to be honest. The choice to let your true self be seen.
Brene Brown
Researcher/Storyteller, USA

Dear Maya,

I am writing this letter on the occasion of your upcoming 13th birthday. First off, I want to say "Happy 13th Birthday Maya!" This is an exciting time in your life where things are changing and you are learning new things. I am so excited for you!

I also wanted you to know how much your mom and dad wanted you, prayed for you and were so joyful when you came into their lives. I remember holding you in my arms when you were about two weeks old, wondering what type of child you would grow up to be. I was so incredibly happy for my dear friends, Gina and Tony, that finally their wish for a precious child had come true. I am glad to say that over the years, I have witnessed you grow into a smart, compassionate, creative and talented young lady. It has been a pleasure watching Gina mother you and to see you now start to stand on your own and exert some independence. While it is hard for a parent to start letting go, we know that we must let go in order for our children to become empowered fully functioning human beings. Be patient with your parents as this time of transition occurs. They love you so very much and want only the best for you. Just remember you have a whole village of people who are always rooting for you every step of the way.

I also wanted to express to you that female centered spaces such as sports teams, clubs, sororities or even friendships are so important. It is an opportunity for you to grow with other young ladies who have the same values, interests and beliefs that you do (that includes your sister, Brooke). Surrounding yourself with that energy is so vitally important in keeping yourself healthy: emotionally, physically, and spiritually. Not to say that being around males does not have value, because it absolutely does. However, there is a power that comes from female centered spaces. I hope as you embark toward adulthood, you will value those spaces. Women are life makers, changers and healers.

You, Maya, are part of that tradition. You are valuable and needed just the way you are. You will grow and change but please remember that who you are is always enough! You don't have to change for anyone but yourself. Those who do not support your growth were not meant to be there for the long haul. I remember someone told me years ago: "People come into your life for a reason, a season or a lifetime." Not everyone is meant to be in your life for a lifetime but you can learn something valuable from all the relationships and encounters you have. Enjoy each day because the present is a gift. What you do with the days you have been given is your gift to the universe.

Again, have a wonderful 13th birthday! I look forward to seeing you enjoy many, many more happy birthdays!! I hope to see you soon!!

Sincerely,
Ms. Ingrid

Dear Maya,

I think the idea of this book is quite clever and I wish I had one at your age. I'm not saying I would've followed the sage advice I was given; youth seems to bring out a stubbornness of always being right. I look back and think of all the things that I wish I had known. I see it as a woman's duty to impart any knowledge or advice she may have to those younger than her. What they do with it is their decision. Below I will explain to you what being a woman means to me and how I managed to traverse through those oh - so difficult years.

The idea of what a woman is supposed to be has been defined by society since the dawn of time. A woman has always been known as the weaker sex, a submissive being. It is only recently that women have been thought of as equals, and the opponents to this thought process still exist. It was less than 100 years ago that women's suffrage was ratified as the 19th amendment. I consider myself blessed, as should you, to be born in a time where the possibilities for our lives are seemingly endless. That's not to say that the fight for equality is over, but we have come a long way. As women, we can take control of our lives and make our own decisions. This means we can make our own way in life, pave our own path, and set the pace. Your life depends on what you want, who you want to be, what kind of woman you are.

A woman to me is someone who is intelligent and looks to expand her knowledge with new experiences. I believe that an education is monumentally important. All around the world young girls are still denied this basic right. Education is your key and will lead you to countless opportunities. You must never feed into the lie that intelligence isn't beautiful. There were girls that I grew up with who went out of their way to make themselves sound ignorant. These girls thought that people wouldn't like them if they were smart. Never sacrifice your intellect to appease others.

I believe a woman is strong because she has to be. You will come in contact with people who want to equate your self-worth with sex. People will tell you that you should be able to cook and keep a house for your husband. Women are often put down when they stray from the ideal of what society has for them. You must be able to stand tall and stay strong in your convictions and be sure of who you are. You must always be vigilant and aware that being a woman means you are vulnerable. As a young girl, I took classes to learn how to protect myself. I highly recommend it. Your strength must come from within. A woman must learn to stand on her own two feet and not to depend on a man. Part of this strength means that you know when to leave a relationship. You should never let anyone put you down.

Artistry is part of womanhood. Every woman enjoys some sort of art form, whether it be singing, painting, or playing an instrument. I think creating something is akin to giving life, which biologically women do. Art is such a vague term that almost anything can be art. Art enriches a woman's life and beautifies the world. By creating something, a woman can pass on a part of herself. My art forms were acting, singing, and writing. I was never as happy as when I was singing. Writing enabled me to express myself and gave me a voice. Acting let me escape my life and take on someone else's. Now art may not be just a part of womanhood, but rather a part of the human experience, a description of the human condition. You can be artistic in hundreds of ways. I advise you to find your craft and nurture it.

Now if I am being honest, I must say that I appreciate being aesthetically pleasing. Although being beautiful isn't just skin deep. I think the most beautiful part of a woman is her heart. Real beauty resonates from the inside. Kindness and humility are stunning and will make people view you as a gorgeous woman. I learned from my mother that helping people is truly rewarding. A beautiful soul is more important than the outside trappings. I'm not saying that you shouldn't be proud of your physicality, but I must stress that inner beauty will make you a prettier person. All women are beautiful. You can be tall or short, fat or thin, you are beautiful. Never change yourself for someone else.

Pride is another part of womanhood. You should be proud of your accomplishments, proud of your personality, proud of being a woman. Religion may sometimes try to deliver a sense of shame to women, making them feel guilty for the crime of being born a female. You must know that you've done nothing to be ashamed of. Being a woman is joyous and should be celebrated. Your body is not unworthy because it is a woman's body. Be proud of what estrogen has given you. As a young adult, I was made to feel like my womanhood was something that should be hidden or down-played. I've grown up to realize that my womanhood is a gift.

There is no right or wrong way to be a woman. I chose intelligence, strength, artistry, beauty and pride because that is what being a woman means to me. Every woman is different and values certain things. Above all I want you to know that being a woman is beautiful and painful.....difficult and enjoyable.......dangerous and wondrous.

Love,
Cousin Jen

Dear Maya,

Happy, happy birthday! How blessed you are to have you mom to collect these words of wisdom from us "elder" ladies! At 13 years old, you will probably read many of these words and smile, but the gravity of meaning may not quite sit with you yet. I was a 13 year old who was in rush to not be a 13 year old for very long. On days that felt yucky and difficult, I was convinced that life would be amazing once I grew up. And I was right----life did end up being utterly amazing in so many ways, but I don't think I took the time to really savor how amazing it had been all along. It's cliche to say I wish I knew then what I know now, because the experiences we have each and every day shape who we become. Even if I could go back in time, I'm pretty sure my stubborn 13 year old self might not believe the things my 40 year old self has to say. But if she would listen for just a minute, the two things I would tell her are this:

1) **Love yourself unconditionally.** As we become women, the world sends us all kind of messages. Some that make us feel strong and beautiful and others that may make our inner voice begin to question these very traits. Sometimes doubt sets in and we wonder if we're good enough, smart enough, pretty enough, athletic enough or enough of whatever we perceive we need to be in that moment. While that voice may get louder with strange new experiences and new people whose paths we cross, you must learn to silence it. You must know that you are always enough. This is what loving yourself is about. It is about taking care of our hearts and our minds and our bodies just as we would for the most precious thing or person that we love outside of ourselves. When we love ourselves, we make decisions that feel right for who we are, we face challenges with courage and most importantly, we share that love with others in a deeper, more connected way. This leads me to number 2....

2) **The most important imprint you will leave in this world is your relationship with others.** One of my favorite Maya Angelou quotes is "I've learned that people will forget what you said, people will forget what you did, but people will never forget how you made them feel." To that I would add, people will forget what you wore, what job you might have had, the haircut you wanted to hide under a hat and whether or not you scored a winning goal. They will forget all of the bad moments you might have a hard time letting go of and they will also forget some of the good. But at the end of it all, they will remember the way you smiled and how it filled them with joy or the love they felt in a hug or the generosity in a kind moment. When you love yourself, you will want to share your light with others and for this they will remember you.

There are many lessons large and small that I could rattle on about, but those are the two that I have come to treasure in my 40th year. I would have liked to learn them a little sooner in my life, so I hope that sharing them with you now, you might think about them from time to time. And just for fun, here are a couple of other bits of wisdom I think about daily:

- Treasure and nurture your friendships. They are one of the most valuable things you will have in this life.
- Always make your bed in the morning as you will be so happy to come home to a tidier room to rest your head after a long day.
- Take 5 minutes each morning to take a few deep breaths before you dive into the madness of the day.
- Whatever it is, it will pass…..eventually. Seriously, it will.
- We are what we think---fill your head with the beautiful things you want your life to be and don't waste time letting your imagination fill you with worry. You can use all of that creativity for far better things!

Have a wonderful birthday Maya. Welcome to our tribe!!

Love,
Ms. Jessica

Every woman who heals herself helps heal all the women who came before her and all the women who came after her.
Dr. Christiane Northrup
Women's Health Advocate, USA

Maya,

Happy 13th birthday! You have reached a milestone in your life, a teenager! I am so proud of you! You are a beautiful young lady!

Here are some thoughts from Bubbie:

Always be interested in everything and everyone! Everyone has a story.

Always ask a question. Then---a second question and maybe even a third!

Always love yourself. You are worthwhile!

Be honest, loyal, trustworthy and trustful, unless that trust is broken.

Smile often.

Always remember the WD40 story and never give up.

Do what you love. Love what you do.

Enjoy your adventure of life!

Life Is Good!

I love you.

Love,
Bubbie

Dearest Maya Joy,

You are 13! How is that even possible? You were my first niece ever. You will always hold a special place in my heart. My own aunts are very special to me and I hope we will always have that same type of bond. No matter what happens----what successes you have, what mistakes you make---I will always have your back and be on your side. You can talk to me about anything. I hope you know that.

I love that your Mom came up with this gift idea for you. She is someone who has taught me a lot since I have known her. Her outlook on life has inspired me to think about the person who I want to be and to consider what gifts I have to offer others.

As you have grown older and have approached this milestone year, I have thought a lot about what advice I might impart to you. I hope you consider my advice with an open mind and an open heart.

<u>You can learn something from every single person you meet.</u> Whether it be the students who you go to school with or your closest friends or your future employers or co-workers or someone who you choose to date or even some random stranger you may meet----every single person has something to offer. Everyone participates in his or her own life journey. And, if you are receptive, you can gather strength from and learn from others' experiences.

The key to learning from others is listening--truly listening--and having an open mind about differing opinions. Not everyone will share the same beliefs as you, but that does not mean that they are wrong and you are right, or vice versa. It just means that differences of opinion exist and that is okay. It would be pretty boring if everyone believed the same thing, looked the same way, and acted the same way. It is in these differences where the learning takes place. You just have to be open and receptive.

There are many people in my life who inspire me and who I have learned from. These are the people who have helped me as I strive to become my very best self. For instance, my Dad is always eager and excited to help other people at the drop of a hat. From him, I have learned that you can receive a lot of joy by helping others. My Uncle Gene has taught me to be generous and loving. Your Mom has shown me the ability to forgive wholly and freely. Your Dad is so dedicated to you and Brooke. I love all his photos----which is the way he shows the world how proud he is of you. Your Uncle Pete always acts with kindness and calmness, even in the most stressful of situations. I love Brooke's huge heart and her love of animals. My 92 year old grandfather, Barnett, is the best listener I know. These are just a few examples of the lessons people have been teaching me. These are the people I want to surround myself with and the characteristics I want to emulate.

There are also people in my life who have made things hard, disappointing and frustrating. But I have learned from these people too. How not to act, how I don't want to be and how I can improve. When life presents obstacles, it is okay to be angry, irritated or to feel overwhelmed. These are necessary emotions.

But how you respond to life's challenges and how you deal with others during the process speaks volumes about the type of person you are. I'm not always perfect, but I try to react to negativity with graciousness and kindness. It's a choice that has served me well even though sometimes I have to force it. Over the years, I have learned that I can only truly control my own actions. Displaying grace and kindness under pressure can really help you to find happiness in the darkest of times.

What people around you have traits that you can learn from? Are they good or maybe not so good? Who do you look up to? Who inspires you? Take their examples and use them to help you become the Maya you are, the Maya you want to be and the Maya you will become.

During our times together, I hope that I have helped you have fun and to be silly. Even when you are old (like me), it's still okay to do headstands all the time, to tell people you love them often and to give hugs and kisses. Don't be afraid to stand up for yourself even when it is uncomfortable. You are always worth it.

You are so smart, loving, tough, athletic, strong, motherly, gorgeous, thoughtful and artistic. I am so proud of you and proud to call you my niece. I will always love you and be here for you. I look forward to spending time with you and to watching you grow into a strong, beautiful woman.

Happy birthday, my sweet Maya Joy. You are loved beyond words!

Love,
Aunt Rebecca

Dear Maya,

It's hard to believe you are turning thirteen! I remember how happy your arrival made your mom and dad and also the rest of your extended family. Now that you are growing up, your mom has asked me to share some advice and thoughts with you.

Well, to tell you the truth, I'm not one for giving advice, but I'll try to share with you some things I have found to be true for me.

Here goes:

- Your family is the most important thing. They will always be there and love you no matter what. Friends come and go, but your family is forever.
- Speaking of friends, choose wisely; a good friend always has your best interest at heart.
- Material things are overrated. It's OK to want more in life, but I have found that the happiness happens when I am content with and grateful for what I have.
- Take joy in the little moments in life.
- A sense of humor is a beautiful thing, especially if you can laugh at yourself occasionally.
- If you have a bad day, stop and take a deep breath. Remember, the next one is usually awesome!
- Be true to yourself and your beliefs/values and everything else will fall into place.
- Oh, and always wear clean underwear. That's important. :)

I wish you all the best, Maya. Life is an amazing journey. Enjoy the ride!

Love,
Aunt Marse

Just look at nature simply. By looking at nature, you can only believe in the existence of something greater than yourself.
Grandmother Bernadette Rebienot, Gabon, Africa
Grandmothers Counsel the World

Dear Maya--

Here are a few of the things I wish I had known when I was your age. The strange thing is, many of these lessons still apply now that I'm an adult, but I sure wish I had known them when I was your age.

- **Listen to your inner voice. Except for when you shouldn't:** This one is tough. We all have a little voice inside that guides us and often helps us to make wise choices. It's important to trust that voice, especially when you know the right thing to do. But here's the thing. You have to know when not to listen to that voice–that's harder. Because sometimes that voice is over-protective and it holds you back from trying new experiences with whispers that you probably won't be good at whatever it is. On those occasions, you need to be stronger than that voice. What is cool is that you *will* know when to listen to it because it's guiding you wisely and when to ignore it because it's holding you back. (Although whether you choose to make a healthy decision is entirely up to you!)
- **Sometimes you're going to suck:** The tricky part is that those whispers that tell you that you might suck at something are often right. I'd say 3 out of 10 times you might really be terrible at something and another 5 out of ten times you'll just be rotten-to-fair (but not terrible). Every once in awhile you'll be pretty good right from the beginning. The thing is, you don't know unless you try. So do it anyway, even if you suck. Because lots of times you'll love doing something, even if you're not great at it. I <u>know</u> that I would have been a cruddy soccer player but I also know I would have loved playing. I regret not taking more risks when I was younger. And it gets harder to do as you get older.
- **"Fear of Trying Things" grows if you feed it. So does "Love of Taking Part in Life"** Emotions are like muscles. The emotions that you feed grow stronger. Those that

you feed by exercising them frequently grow bigger and stronger. The emotions you tamp down tend to wither and eventually starve. You get to decide which emotions you want to feed. If the emotion that you are tending to most closely is fear or anxiety, that is the one that will start to rule your decision-making process. On the flip side, if you make a decision that you are going to push through the anxiety and try new experiences, you will grow in a multitude of ways. You'll grow your ability to take a risk without the fear of failing. You'll have a world of experiences that you would otherwise miss. You'll learn an incredible amount about yourself and what you're capable of doing. And I guarantee you that you are capable of so much more than you know. So take a risk...

But not all risks are worth it........

Smoking leads to lung cancer.

Drinking and driving (or getting in the car with someone who is drinking and driving) is a deadly combination. You would not be able to live with the consequences if you were to hurt or kill someone because you drove while drinking.

Loads of teens send naked pictures of themselves to people they like. I know that sounds repulsive to you right now and maybe it will still sound like a terrible idea a few years from now. I'd like to think that you'll always know that it's a bad idea. I'm just mentioning it because, believe it or not, a lot of really smart kids I know make dumb decisions when it comes to love. Those pictures always get out. THEY NEVER DON'T GET FORWARDED TO OTHER PEOPLE! (You can see I'm trying hard to emphasize that because sometimes when our heart is making decisions, it blinds you to that inner wise voice). That brings us to romance...

- **Everything Happens When it's Supposed To (especially if you're taking advantages of those opportunities that come to you)** You will absolutely, 100%, without fail get breasts, get your period and get a boyfriend or a girlfriend (depending on where your heart leads you). These life events won't necessarily happen for you at the same time they do for everyone else, but they will happen. So try not to worry about any of them all too much. Love the moment that you are in. Remember to enjoy this time because once it is over, you never get it back (and, as I said, everything will happen in time, even if you're not obsessing about it).

- **About Where Your Heart Might Lead You** I don't know if you will find yourself falling in love with a boy or another girl. You might not know yet either. That can raise a lot of questions and worries. Falling in love can be a confusing thing (Especially when everyone assumes they know who you're going to love and even you don't know who you're going to love--or sometimes you **do** know who you're attracted to but it's different from who everyone thinks you're going to be attracted to). Not to mention that sometimes who you're attracted to changes depending on the person. Here's the thing; you don't have to have it all figured out (besides, just when you think you have it all figured out, the answers might change). But ultimately, love is love and who you love is up to you. I just want to mention that it might not occur to the adults in your life that you might fall in love with someone they're not expecting. That doesn't mean it isn't ok with them–it might just mean that they grew up at a time when things were less fluid and they didn't realize that it was ok to be a "he" or a "she" or a "they" if that's what felt right to them. (Let's be honest, they might not know it even now unless you open that door and have that conversation with them. But adults are human too and sometimes they'll need you to introduce new ideas to them.

Have the conversation with them. Give them a chance to love you just the way you are).

- **About Romance** Boyfriends and girlfriends are wonderful but so are friends. This is a biggie—if I could go back and re-do one thing from my younger days (which I can't because once a moment is over you never get it back), I'd focus less on the boys I liked and more on the girls I liked. With any luck, you'll have many romantic relationships—and a few of them might be long-term relationships with wonderful partners. But most of those relationships will eventually end and you will move on. It's pretty rare that these people remain in our lives (even the wonderful ones that you can't imagine living without). And, by the way, I am so grateful that I didn't marry any of the boys I cried my eyes out over! When I look back at the guys I was hopelessly in love with, there isn't a single one I can imagine spending my life with. To tell you the truth, there aren't many I can remember at all! (But since those relationships are going to end, remember what I said and don't send naked pictures of yourself.)

- **Each relationship teaches you something about yourself and what's important to you.** Never compromise what's important to you for someone else—girl or guy. True friends won't ask that of you. And since most romances are going to end...

- **Focus on your friends** Too many teens spend all of their time thinking about their boyfriends or girlfriends and forget about their other friends when they are dating someone. That's a really big mistake. Your friends are there for life (you don't have to marry them or choose just one). Grow your friendships. Water them with time and attention. Friends are the greatest gift you can ask for.

- **"Balance" Matters Most** There are many wonderful opportunities that are likely to come your way. Experience them all (take those risks) but not at the same time. Keep balance in your life so that there is always time for family, friends, self, work and play. You need all of them. At different times, different ones will take precedence, but there is never a time when you shouldn't strive to have a little bit of all of them in your life.

- **Work hard to do well (whether you end up doing well or not).** Good grades don't matter–but working hard for good grades does. You will always be able to look at the effort you put in and feel proud if you know that you've given it your all. Sometimes an A means very little when you know you didn't work hard for it. And sometimes that B means everything when you know that you had to work your butt off to get it. "Working hard" is another muscle that you want to develop for life. And, trust me, there are a million colleges that would be great places to end up. You'll get into a bunch of them no matter what your grades are. Everyone who truly wants to get into college, gets into college. And it will be a great college! But the habits you develop now will determine how you do later. So start to work on working hard (that one might be more a reminder to myself than to you...)

- **Love the work you choose** There are a lot of terrific careers out there. Some pay more than others. You are going to spend more time at your job than just about anything else in your adult life. Try to choose something you feel good about and love doing, even if it doesn't pay the most.

- **Life always gets better (and if it doesn't, you're not doing something right)** In my humble opinion, you are going through some of the tougher parts of life around now. There are a lot of decisions that you don't get to make for yourself (like whether you want to study chemistry or not). You *do* get to decide how you're going to respond to what life demands though. Choose to make the most of your time and make it the best experience it can be. And when a situation seems intolerable, ask yourself whether it will still matter in a day or a week. That often helps you gain good perspective.

BUT, I truly believe that life gets better as you get older. You will have more freedom to make choices about how you spend your time and energy. That's why it's important to choose to add positive experiences and people to your life. If your life isn't all that you wish it were, then you have the power to change it. Never forget that.

- **Be Kind** That's just a good one to keep in mind. It is never the wrong decision to treat someone with kindness. It never backfires or leads you astray. So that's just basic good advice. When you're stuck and not sure how to respond to someone, choose kindness. After all, if you still want to be mean and spiteful later, you can always go back and act that way later. It's easy to undo kindness. On the other hand, if you choose ugly now, it's harder to take back!
- **Get Enough Sleep** Lots of science shows that our brain cells regenerate while we're sleeping AND that while we're sleeping, the cells in our brains shrink, allowing the cerebrospinal fluid to seep in around the cells and bathe our brain in goodness, washing away harmful toxins. Bet you didn't see that one coming, huh? But yes, sleep is high on my list of good advice (even if it's at the end of this list). Also, sleep is a good brake to impose on yourself before you make any big decision (like whether to be mean or kind, or whether to go out on a date on Friday night or hang out with your friends, or whether to exercise your Fear Muscle or your Love of Taking Part in Life muscle, or whether you should send that naked picture of yourself–I'm

only emphasizing that one because no one else is going to remember to tell you about that!)

I'm sure there are lots more pieces of wisdom that I could share but these are the ones that rank pretty high on my list.

Love,
Ms. Robyn

Maya,

I'm so excited for you, stepping across the bridge from childhood to another stage in your life. Some of those steps will be sure and bold, while others will be a little hesitant. Be sure to keep some of the special "childlike" parts of your life. They will help you to decide which new friends and experiences you wish to accept and the paths you wish to travel.

Some of this change and growth will be difficult but always know you have family and friends to support you and the result will make you stronger and able to meet life's challenges with confidence.

Enjoy the journey!

Love,
Mom Mom

She is clothed with strength and dignity, and
she laughs without fear of the future.
Proverbs 31:25 New Living Translation
Christianity

Dear Maya,

As I think back on the years and the challenges that I faced when I was a teenager, knowing what I know now, I wish there were some things I could have told my younger self. I hope you will really take these things in and carry them with you as you approach womanhood.

First, I'd like to remind you that you are so very PRECIOUS. Precious is defined as "of great value, not to be wasted or treated carelessly." Your whole being is to be cherished and you are a gift. There will be many people who intend to use you for their own needs or wants. You would never give diamonds or rubies to just anyone to do just anything. You are worth far more than jewels. I advise you to never allow someone to treat you with disregard and never allow anyone to take advantage of you. You get to show people how they should treat you by treating yourself as precious and valuable.

Another solid piece of wisdom is knowing that "what other people think of me is none of my business." The quote is attributed to several people, so I'm not sure from whom it originated. I just know it is an amazing little nugget to carry with you. As you are discovering who you are, even at this age, you know some things about yourself. Stand firm in those things. You know who you are, where you are strong and where it would serve you to improve. No one should be able to convince you differently--whether it is as trivial as someone expressing that they think your hair or wardrobe is not right or as big as an attack on your character, it is not your concern what anybody else decides to focus on or make up about you. Know what you know about you. Be strong and confident in that. The traits you develop now can likely stick with you and help shape your life's direction. Choose wisely.

You will fall in love. The first heartbreak is tough. It will pass (pretty quickly). Be bold enough to open your heart over and over again to fully experience each relationship. Each love will teach you and help you to grow. The pain of loss is temporary and a natural part of grieving the end of a relationship. It's perfectly ok. With the close of one relationship is the opening of many opportunities for new direction.

Maya, life will take you through many joys and many challenges. Each of those experiences, whether painful or pleasurable, will help you become the woman you were designed to be. When you live your life with good character, all things will ultimately work together for your good. It's all coming together for the betterment of you, even the tough stuff. Good or bad, it will pass. You will stand stronger for going through it. Blessings sometimes feel like joy and other times feel like pressure. God loves us enough to give us what we need and not what we want. Remember, no matter what, life is working in your favor.

Be great Lady Maya! The world needs you!

Love,
Ms. Raina

Maya,

Always keep the sparkle in your eyes and your uplifting spirit. Life is a journey with highs and lows along the way. However, continue to keep your goals in the forefront. Your family loves you and will always be there to support you in your efforts.

Love Always,
Memere

Thousands of candles can be lit from a single candle
and the life of the candle will not be shortened.
Happiness never decreases by being shared.
Translation of the Sutra of 42 Sections
Buddhism

Dear Maya,

When I think of my teen years, a smile brightens up my mind. Except for my stint with pneumonia during the summer of my sophomore year, I was a healthy young lady. I went to and from high school with friends from St. Ursula School. I felt very accepted by my friends. We worked hard to help one another over the challenges of failing grades, disappointing boyfriends and our relationships with our family, especially our parents.

Somehow it was easier to be a part of the family before reaching those years that end with "teen." But I knew being in right relationship with my family, even the extended members, was very, very important.

It was during this time that I realized that God was calling me to join the Sisters who were teaching at St. Ursula. I really didn't want to go, but I knew if I didn't I would not be a happy camper. And as a consequence, I have been a very, very happy camper.

But that's a theme for another time!

Keep loving and you will be okay.

Love,
Great Aunt Barbara

Dear Maya,

You are a beautiful, smart, talented, athletic and artistic niece. It has been so wonderful to watch you blossom and grow over the past 13 years.

Being 13 is such a special time in a girl's life. 13 is the start of becoming more independent. 13 is having the freedom to explore new interests. 13 is choosing new paths in your journey toward adulthood. 13 is about making lasting memories with friends. 13 is about becoming a woman. 13 is such an exciting time in your life. 13 is so, so special my lovely niece.

With all of the bright joy, laughter and fun of 13, sometimes being a teenager and growing into the woman that you will become can feel emotional and complicated too. During these times, I want you to remember that no matter what others say and do, always be you. Follow your dreams and always be you. Always remember that you are wonderful just the way you are.

Uncle Dave, Cousin Liam and I are very proud of you! We are always here for you. We love you very much, Maya.

Keep shining!

Love,
Aunt Mirella

Dear Maya,

I was so honored when your Mom asked me to be a part of your special gift. It took me only a minute to remember when I was your age and about four beautiful women who had a lasting impact on my life. One of these women was my own Mom and the rest of them were members of our church. They were all dearest friends. They were all career women with important jobs, beautiful homes and the latest style clothes. I wanted so much to be like them when I grew up with all those "things" but they would teach me that while all those outward things were wonderful, who we are on the inside is so much more important and lasting than what we have on the outside.

You see their inner beauty was what made them so successful. They were good and kind, loving, giving, patient, joyful, gentle, faithful and humble. They all had a very deep faith and they lived their faith everyday. I loved these women and to this day remember what they taught me about "inner beauty."

It is my prayer for you that God will bless your life with wonderful women also who will help you nurture your inner beauty, for when you do, you will be successful in your life.

In ancient times, the ruby was the most valued and precious of all gemstones. There is a verse in the Bible that says "A woman of noble character (inner beauty) is worth far more than rubies." How beautiful is that!

Happy Birthday Maya!

Love,
Aunt Connie

Wherever you turn, there is the face of God.
Qur'an 2:114
Islam

Dear Maya,

Here are some words of advice:

Don't give into pressure to dumb yourself down! Especially for a boy or to fit in with a crowd. As smart women, we do this too often.

Ask for what you need while respecting the needs of others. Be your own best advocate! As gentle women, we don't do this often enough.

Avoid over-apologizing! As women, we do this too often. We must remember that an apology isn't an apology unless it is meaningful.

Happy 13th birthday!

With Love,
Your Cousin Jessica

I have met brave women who are exploring the outer edge of human possibility, with no history to guide them, and with a courage to make themselves vulnerable that I find moving beyond words.
Gloria Steinham
Political Activist, USA

Maya,

Since this is a significant birthday, I just wanted to tell you a few important things that I've learned through the years!

First......No one will ever love you the way your Mom and Dad love you.

Second......Be grateful and tell your loved ones you love them every chance you get.

Third......Focus on your studies, stick to your goals, play to win, enjoy life and value yourself always.

Congratulations on becoming a teenager! Your 13th birthday is as special as you are, Maya! So be the best teenager you can be!

Happy 13th Birthday Maya!!!

Love,
Aunt Denise

Surround yourself with only people who
are going to lift you higher.
Oprah Winfrey
Entrepreneur/Philanthropist, USA

Dear Maya,

It is hard to believe that you are turning thirteen. This is such an amazing part of life and I am happy to share some advice with you as you enter your teenage years.

- Always be kind and respectful to others.
- Just be yourself. Don't worry what others think and don't try and change yourself for someone else.
- Realize that it is ok to make a mistake.
- Keep a journal and take notes. I wish I would have done that. It would have been so great to go back and read my thoughts as a teen.
- Most importantly, enjoy life and appreciate all the beautiful things around you.

I wish you the best on your birthday.

Love,
Cousin Christie

We do not see things as they are. We see things as we are.
Talmud
Judaism

Dear Maya,

When your Mom requested input to be included in your Birthday Book, she suggested that we might want to share an experience from teenage years. Unfortunately, I do not have many positive experiences from that time in my life. The environment in which I grew up was not one conducive to such experiences. What I remember from that time is the feeling of the need to hide and survive. I share this with you because I want to express how truly grateful I am that this has not been your experience. You have been blessed with two parents who work hard to provide you with the love and support that each child needs and deserves. I know that sometimes, in the moment, it is difficult to remember all of the love that has been given, all the guidance that has been offered and all of the help that has been provided.

Even though my early life experience was very different from yours, I am grateful that I survived, which then allowed me to grab the opportunities that life has offered me since that time in my life. I am truly blessed and just wanted to let you know that no matter what life gives us, we can move through each situation and grow from it. There is always support available, from both seen and unseen sources. From my life experience, I have come to believe that the Universe provides us with absolutely everything needed to not only survive, but to thrive.

This is my wish for you. Please know that you are always surrounded by Light and Love. That even though bad things may happen, which they will, all will be well. The Universe wants us to shine who we truly are to everyone we come in contact with. The other side of that is to be aware of the light that shines from everyone with whom we come in contact.

As you move into this next phase of your life, Blessings and Peace be with you. You are a beautiful, accomplished child of the Eternal.

With so much Love,
Aunt Loretta

The splendor of the rose and the whiteness of the lily do not rob the little violet of its scent not the daisy of its simple charm. If every flower wanted to be a rose, spring would lose its loveliness.
Therese de Liseux
Christian Saint, France

Happy 13th Birthday Maya!

It is so exciting to be a teenager! I remember my 13th birthday and feeling so excited! I was finally able to see PG-13 movies and could read teen magazines!

As you turn 13, don't wish you could be or do anything else. Love each day and have fun in it! I look back and realized I spent a lot of time wishing I was older. I feel now that I lost a lot of time doing this because I wasn't enjoying where I was and what I was doing in that moment.

The gift of this book from your mom is that it collects a lot of wisdom. We learn so much from others. It gives you a lot of insight to think about---but mostly it highlights that there are lots of choices in life. <u>Always choices!</u>

You are the author of your life. Your choices make it as exciting, fun, interesting, and adventurous as you want it to be. And that is key---WHAT YOU WANT IT TO BE! You are the creator--so do everything for you, because you like it, or because you want it, or because it matters to YOU.

Listen to your heart---feel with your whole self--know that all your answers are within you. Be patient with yourself and with those around you. Be kind to yourself and those around you. Have compassion for yourself and those around you. And have fun! Laugh. Laugh. Laugh. And laugh some more!

We are here on this Earth to enjoy and feel great! So always do what makes you feel great!

I am so excited to be in your life and am always here for you---to cheer you on, to celebrate you and to just listen if you want to talk.

YOU are an amazing, beautiful, intelligent, creative, fun, athletic, marvelous, adorable and awesome young lady! And I thank you for all the greatness you bring to the world---just as you are! Always love and be your wonderful, true self!

With nothing but love for you always,
Aunt Heather

Dear Maya,

You have been born with special gifts. There is no one in the whole world exactly like you! Be true to yourself and keep an open heart. You will become aware of these gifts as you grow older. The world needs you!

As you grow older, never forget the little girl you started out as, for she will stay with you even as you gain more years. Go forth and be the awesome girl you are and the woman you are becoming!

You are strong and beautiful!

With love and hugs,
Ms. Sarah

As a Grandmother speaking for my grandchildren and for the next seven generations, I feel we must see how we are all mirrors for each other. White people ask me how I can love them and I say because I can see myself in you. Grandmother Margaret Behan, Arapahoe-Cheyenne, USA <u>*Grandmothers Counsel the World*</u>

Dearest Maya,

You don't know me very well, but I have known your Mom since she was born. She is a wonderful lady and she picked a wonderful man for her husband.

As you begin a new phase in your life, embrace every minute. Hold onto the memories.

Mom and Dad will be in your life as you go through all of the phases. Love them, cherish them and listen to them. You will have many friends who enter your life, but none will be as faithful, wise and loving as your parents.

I love you and am looking forward to watching you grow into adulthood and hope to attend your wedding down the road.

Happy 13th birthday Maya!!!

Love,
Aunt Weez

First we do things, later we understand.
Na'aseh v'nishma
Judaism

Birthday Blessing, sweet Maya!

I AM so honored your mom asked me to contribute to your birthday book!

First I would like to share why birthdays are so special! Each birthday, the sun returns to the exact place in the sky when you took your first breath; it's called your solar return. Another reason your birthday is a very special day is because your guides and angels are especially close. On this day, they celebrate your soul, they come closer so you can commune with them and receive their blessings and guidance for your new year. It's a good day to take time to be still and listen. Feel how loved you are.

I remember when I met you and Brooke. Do you remember? We meditated and played with the tuning forks. Roxy and Mr. Pumpkin, my orange cat, were so happy to play with you. I remember how wise beyond your years you were then. I can imagine how beautifully your soul has blossomed.

That is the image I AM being guided to share with you Maya. *"You are an eternal Flower of Love. Each incarnation or lifetime your soul unfurls more petals releasing your unique beauty to the world."* Meditate on this image each year on your solar return and you will see the beautiful expressions of you ready to be expressed.

As with earthly flowers, your soul requires nourishment to flourish. As you grow in years, you will have many opportunities to learn how to care for your soul. This is the most important relationship to nurture. When you cultivate an intimate relationship with your soul, you will always recognize your voice of truth in any given moment.

Remember you have the power of choice Maya. Your life is your own. You came here to have your own unique experience. You have chosen a beautiful family to share this journey of life. My greatest gift to you dear one, is to remind you to ENJOY ALL OF LIFE. Trust that every choice you make adds to your life experiences and all are perfect for you. Your JOY in life is water for your soul.

You may wonder "what is the soul?" and that is a good question. The answer is yours to remember. Beginning each day with gratitude asking these questions will guide you to discover the voice of your soul.

"How shall I live today?"
"How shall I create today?"
"How shall I love today?"
"How shall I injoy today?"

Infinite blessings to you sweet love!

All Love,
Ms. Liz

Happy 13th Birthday Maya!

You have grown up to be such a strong, confident and self-reliant person. I am so proud of you because you don't give in to peer pressure. You don't care about what other people think, especially if someone pokes fun at you!

I remember a time when I was 13. My dad took me to a party and there were younger kids there and older kids there and I didn't fit in. I didn't know what to do, so I pretended to look for a necklace that I lost. I didn't really lose a necklace, but it gave me something to do at the party. Awkward!

I also remember my niece at her middle school dance when I danced with her! I don't get why 13 year olds get so embarrassed dancing, unless it's the dab! If you say the word "awkward", it isn't so "awkward".

You have already experienced so much in life and are very appreciative of it! Your family loves you very much! If it takes more than 365 days to get to 14, then there is something wrong! LOL!

Happy 13th birthday! Have fun!

Ms. Susan

Dear Maya,

Happy 13th Birthday and welcome to womanhood! It has been a joy to watch you grow up (mostly through Facebook, since I live in Florida). The relationship you have with your sister Brooke and cousin Liam is very sweet and I hope it continues to grow as you all do.

I wasn't really sure what to write when your Mom asked me about contributing. On one hand, your parents have been so supportive that I feel like they have probably given you any advice I could think of. On the other hand, my teen years were some of the most difficult for me personally, so I wasn't sure how I could give advice at this time in your life. And then I realized the biggest thing I would tell you is what I regularly need to tell myself - stop judging. This letter will be what it is, just like our lives are filled with a mix of wonder and awkwardness.

So, here are my wishes and words of wisdom for you as you embark on adulthood:

1. Be gentle with yourself. You will make mistakes and you will do beautiful things. You will get pimples and crushes. You may struggle with body image or you might be truly happy with yourself - there is no shame in either. There is also no shame in both happening on the same day. We are creatures with emotions; these things happen. No matter what you do in life, you are not the best or the worst, so be gentle.

2. Believe in something. I was raised Catholic, but when I was about your age I started to questions things. I felt on the outside of the church, like I did not belong. When I was 17, I met a wonderful woman who became a mentor to me. She took me to a Native American sweat lodge, a synagogue, a mosque, and various Christian

churches. We meditated, went on a silent weekend retreat, and at the end of each experience, she would have me write down what I liked. She helped me to piece together my concept of God through these experiences. It was beautiful and so helpful. I realized that it doesn't matter who or what I believe in, but belief helps me feel part of the universe, loved, and cared for by something bigger than myself. I'm not sure about your experience with religion, but I hope you know and feel that you are a part of something bigger.

3. Take your time. This applies to so many things in life.

A. The awkward one first: sex. Most adults will tell you they wish they had waited until they were older before having sex. Teens are in a crazy rush to become adults, and it's just not necessary. Enjoy the steps along the way. Holding hands is sweet. Kissing is awesome. Talking is one of the most intimate things you can do. And talk to your Mom; she might feel awkward, but she loves you and wants the best for you.

B. Less awkward: school. AP classes are great, but so is having a life. I have seen many of my students exhaust themselves with AP, sports, Debate, etc. and not really get to enjoy high school. No matter which path you choose, make time to enjoy yourself. College is the same. Everyone's path is different. One of my best friends finished his Bachelor's degree in 3 years, went on to law school, and became a partner in a law firm at 26 (huge accomplishment). I used to judge myself because I had a different path. I tried school full time, but struggled with structure and didn't do well. My path was working full time and going to school part time. This allowed me to focus on classes, gain work experience, and discover what I really wanted to do. It wasn't just about grades; I was really able to enjoy my classes and this helped me graduate with a great GPA.

C. In the future: marriage and kids. You may have noticed a pattern here, but there are many paths to getting married and having kids. There isn't a timeline or necessity for marriage. Your parents have a beautiful and long marriage. They grew up together. My parents got married when they were 21 and 22, so I thought I should do that, too. I was DEFINITELY not ready at that age, and I'm glad I waited. My parents got divorced, which I said I would never do, but I did. I have always wanted children, and after being married for 3 years, my husband realized he didn't. It was heartbreaking, but I knew I wouldn't be happy if I stayed with him. He is a good person, and I still care for him, but I am also about to adopt this year. There is no perfect way to get married and have kids, including the fact that you don't have to do either if you don't feel that is right for you.

4. Find joy. There are big and small things in every day that can be appreciated, and it is important to focus on those things. You don't have to ignore problems, but finding joy, being grateful, and focusing on the beauty in life will help you face your difficulties. At times, my job is really annoying, but every day there is at least one kid who I am happy to see and know I have helped. Some days I am lonely, and my dog snuggles up next to me (then usually farts). My Mom has struggled with her health over the years, so my Dad and other family members are even more precious to me. Some people have hardships in life and let those pull them down into negativity and depression. I have struggled with depression since childhood, so I insist on finding joy in everyday, and it makes my life full and better.

Much love,
Your cousin Bronwen

Maya,

Turning 13 is the transition from a child to becoming a teenager/ young lady. You are maturing mentally and it can be a very emotional time in your life. Maybe playing with dolls is no longer fun, but giggling all the time with your friends will be the new fun. As well as love for all things and people, why people act the way they do, why my body is changing just to name a few. Don't want to scare you! LOL!

At 13, I wished I listened more to my elders who gave me advice. You think you know everything, but in reality you are still learning!

Being a woman to me means:

*CONFIDENCE
*HAVING A GIVING SPIRIT
*KNOWING YOUR WORTH
*BEING GROUNDED IN YOUR SPIRITUALITY

The beautiful part of being a woman is we are nurturers. We hold everything together with the support of our family.....FAMILY ALWAYS COMES FIRST. And we love unconditionally. As you turn 13, you will feel like your mom is the enemy ("No you can't go to that party" "No you cannot date yet") but she is not the enemy. She is your BEST AND ONLY FRIEND WHO WILL BE THERE FOR YOU NO MATTER WHAT, PERIOD.

Maya you are very fortunate to have great parents who love you and each other. They have set high standards for any young man to hold up to once you start dating. Accept nothing less. Your role models are right there in your own home. You never have to look outside of your home for a role model. Gina and Tony "got it on lock."

May you live life to the fullest and be the BEST MAYA YOU CAN BE. The world is waiting on you! Enjoy the Rollercoaster Ride called LIFE!

Love you,
Auntie Jackie

For the sake of it, you journey to sacred shrines and holy rivers, but this priceless jewel is within your own heart.
Guru Granth Sahib
Sikhism

Precious Maya,

First and foremost your name defines your journey to greatness. The definition of Maya---the power by which the universe becomes manifest; the illusion or appearance of the phenomenal world. The most beautiful, angelic, ambrosial, enticing, gorgeous, enamoring, pretty, amazing, lovely, lovable, and wonderful girl anyone could ever meet.

What I remember about turning 13......
Here's what I do remember:
I remember my hormones out of whack.
I remember feeling like my Mom was from another planet (the meanest one).
I remember finding true friendships.
I remember feeling relieved that my friends had the same doubts and fears as I did.
I remember looking at the boys a little differently.
I remember truly caring about how I dressed or wore my hair.
I remember feeling a bit confused on my purpose in life.
I remember having fun, laughing for no reason.
I remember feeling so thankful my friends felt the same way I did.

And most of all I remember feeling I was not alone.

Here's what I want you to remember:
Remember to choose friends who are good to you.
Remember to cherish each and every relationship.
Remember your parents were once 13 and sometimes make mistakes, but love you unconditionally.
Remember to study hard and strive for excellence.
Remember it's OK to fail as long as you learn from your mistakes.
Remember you are truly beautiful no matter what anyone says.
Remember to remain thankful.
Remember to laugh and have fun.

Remember you are a gift to any relationship.
Remember you are still a teen and it's OK to be ultra silly. You'll
grow up soon enough.

And most of all remember you are not alone.

Now it is my time to speak favor over you Maya......

Dear Father in Heaven,

We humbly come before you today and ask that you watch over our
precious Maya. We praise your name and thank you for allowing
Maya to see her 13th birthday. Please allow her to see how great and
powerful she is. Help her to always have mentors to guide through to
adulthood. Heavenly Father we ask for you to guide her through this
journey, continuing to grow into the most beautiful woman inside
and out. We thank you Lord for giving her such great parents and
a strong foundation. God we ask for you to reign blesing on Maya
and bless her beyond her wildest dreams. In Jesus Christ's name,
Amen, Amen, Amen.

Maya, I have a daughter named Amaya (also influenced by Maya
Angelou) and son Makai born on March 25, 2004. So I have felt
a deep connection to you from the first time your mom and I
discussed details of our families. You will always have a light shining
in my heart.

Love,
Ms. Alita

Dear Maya,

Happy, Happy 13th birthday to you! Starting your "teens" is such an exciting time of life. It's a big transition from childhood to young adulthood. To commemorate this, your Mom reached out to many relatives, friends and important and even famous people of our time asking them to contribute to this compilation of stories, thoughts and advice which may help you as you turn this significant corner in your life. I feel very honored to have been asked to be a part of this group and to be a part of your celebration.

First, I want to take a moment to acknowledge you as a person, just as you are this day. I get to spend a lot of time with your Mom and love hearing all the wonderful stories she shares with me about you. I have been so lucky and happy to personally watch you grow up for several years now. I will never forget the time we went camping together and you faced a big challenge of going up to the snack stand and ordering your own ice cream. I know that was just a small event and you may not even remember that day, but to me, that was such a big day in my awareness of you. I was so proud of you because I knew it was a struggle and yet you persevered. You took those tremulous steps and got through the challenge. From that day, it seems to me, you have continued to grow in your strength and your confidence. You have become more and more aware of the things you like and what makes Maya, Maya. I love your love of all things Harry Potter, your determination and commitment to soccer, your dedication to your studies and drive to excellence in all things. You are a strong, smart, beautiful and loving girl and I have no doubt that these traits will stay with you and continue to grow as you take each step toward becoming a woman.

So now it is my time to offer some words of wisdom or at least share with you the lessons I have learned in life thus far (because we are always students of life). Two mottos that my Mom has shared with me and I find to be true and have served me well are:

1) **"Everything in Moderation"**-- You can enjoy all kinds of things, and passion should not be ruled out, but it's good to enjoy the pleasures in life in moderation so that they don't take up all the time of being. So, in other words, keep things in balance....live, love, work.

2) **"What's For You Doesn't Miss You"**--This motto deals more with the heart and disappointments. Things seem to hit us much harder when we're younger. Throughout my life, disappointments seem to have started out as mountains, but are now more like molehills. I do have a sense that things in life work out for the best. Perhaps there's a situation you may want to happen a certain way or there may be an item you really want to have...whatever it may be that you have your sights set on many not happen as you want it to happen. However, down the road, you realize that things did really work out for the best. That would be my hope for you, that you don't have to experience too much disappointment and that any difficult situation turns around and you get to appreciate that the turn that it took was for the best.

These sayings are really from my Mom although I have adapted them for my own life. It's hard to narrow down ideas and quotes to share with you, but I will add one that has struck me recently. It's from the Phantom Tollbooth by Norton Juster. As a teacher, I love this book. I think it offers a lot of life wisdom about keeping things in perspective and in balance and about courage. Here is one of my favorite quotes: *"Many places you would like to see are just off the map and many things you want to know are just out of sight or a little beyond your reach. But someday you'll reach them all, for what you learn today, for no reason at all, will help you discover all the wonderful secrets of tomorrow."*

I like this quote because it speaks to the fact that everything that you are doing now plays a part in who you will be in the future. Not to put pressure on you, but rather to understand that you can enjoy everything, successes and failures, joys and sorrows, ease and difficulty because it will all lead you to where you are going. It's your original path and only you can make it. I also like it because it coincides with the road you are on of discovery and knowledge. There is a whole huge world of wonderful out there. Enjoy all the moments and experiences you are creating today as they lead you to the amazing time of tomorrow.

I wish you all the success and the ability to reach for all you desire. You are a gifted young lady with a strong, supportive family and fantastic friendships. I look forward to watching the path that you will take and sharing in the joy you will experience in taking it.

With all the love in my heart,
Ms. Gigi

Dearest Maya,

13?! Wow--time flies. You are such a beautiful young lady already and shine with such a light that will undoubtedly make such a difference in the world. I have personally seen that already since you were a mere elementary-aged girl. There are a few things that I have learned along the way in my own lifetime that I would love to pass along to my 13 year old self if I had the chance to do so, so instead I will impart some of these ideas on you.

One is this saying "Every stage of your life requires a different version of yourself." What that means to me in relation to being new to the teenage world is that this is your opportunity to discover who "yourself" actually is. I believe we evolve over our lifetimes, but at the core, we are always the same being. So the first step is to discover who "Maya" is and then build from there. This is the time you get to try on different hats and find things that spark you. These things that call to you will always be things you can come back to as you grow...but try things that are beyond your comfort zone too. Because this is the time that you can!

I've joked with Brady recently that people will always use the phrase "you're acting like such a teenager!" as you grow older and even into adulthood. So go ahead now and act like one while you have the authority to be able to do so! Being a teenager is a time of self-discovery is what I am trying to say I guess.....use it wisely! And while you will evolve and grow and become a different version of yourself along the way like that saying goes (maybe even day by day), knowing who you are at the core will always bring you back to home base. And learning who you are at the core this early on? That will only help you. So lean on those wise people around you. (You have so many!). Be introspective. Have fun with your friends. Act a little crazy. It's all part of it!!

Above all, enjoy the journey Maya. I can't wait to see what roads you pave going forward. You are already a remarkable young lady and will surely grow into someone even more incredible as the years go on. Wishing you lots of love and success darling!

XOXO--

Ms. Kim

Girls should never be afraid to be smart.
Emma Watson
Actress/Activist for Civil Rights, USA

Dear Maya,

Happy 13th birthday!! I am honored to be a part of your special day by participating in this book you mom is putting together. I met your mom at Tai Sophia. I think this book is a grand idea! I hope you think so too.

My birthday wish for you is to encourage you to be adventurous and say yes to new experiences, draw outside of the box and follow your own path, especially if your friends or peers don't think it's cool or popular. Have the courage to be who you are!

When I look back at when I was 13, I remember that at times it was very hard to do and wish I had been braver. It took me awhile to befriend, accept and embrace my inner me, instead of hiding my interests and opinions that were different from others, especially my friends. Listen to your own wisdom and if something doesn't feel right, follow that as well. When you are not sure, seek out good people who are wise and listen deeply so you can figure out what to do or not do and to be true to yourself.

Learn from your mistakes. I find that seeing them as lessons and gifts has really helped me and made them easier to accept and acknowledge. I also think it has been important to learn balance and to not take myself so seriously. Treasure the people you love! Take good care of yourself on your journey in life. Surround yourself with people that have positive energy. And when times are hard, turn to your friends and family for comfort and warmth.

Wishing you another year around the sun full of love, laughter and lightness!

Fondly,
Ms. Mary

At the edge of the cornfield, a bird will sing with them in the oneness of their happiness. So they will sing together with the universal power, in harmony with the one Creator of all things. And the bird song, and the people song and the song of life will become one.
Song of the Long Hair Kachinas
Hopi Tribe, USA

Dear Maya,

Happy birthday. How lovely to be asked to participate in a celebration of you. I also bow to your mom's wisdom. She knows that a young woman benefits and thrives from the support, experience and wisdom of other women. In many cultures, you already would be considered a woman. And if you lived among some indigenous people, you might have "spiritual godmothers" to provide guidance along your way.

What I've learned in my 70 times around the sun is that I carry a treasure within me. I have a treasure map that points me to the gold. I know I carry the cycles of nature within me. This knowledge is mine and it is yours too. You carry the depth of the ocean and the flows of the rivers and streams. Let water remind you to be fluid and powerful. You carry the creative force of the springtime. Let the plants and trees remind you to grow and be strong and flexible. You radiate the warmth of the summer sun. You flourish and help other flourish. Let that warmth overflow and remind you to have joy and laughter and give it away with generosity. The sun shines on everyone. You carry the late summer's great bounty and abundance within you. You have the ability to support, nourish and care for others; and at the same time, care for yourself. Let the beauty of the earth remind you of all the gifts you have been given. Let yourself know your value. Let yourself acknowledge your own uniqueness. Treat yourself and others with honor and integrity. Your life is precious and finite. Just like a glorious tree in the autumn.

These gifts are your birthright. They can never be taken away. You've had them from your very first breath and will have them until the day you take your last breath. I send you much love and a big welcome.

Love,
Ms. Susan

If you are grateful, I will surely increase you in favor.
Qur'an 14:7
Islam

Dear Maya,

On the occasion of your 13th birthday, here are some thoughts I hope will be useful for your journey into your teenage years and adulthood.

You have a loving, peaceful family who will always be your best guide and source of support, but always know you have many, many people to help you if you ever need us!

Your teenage years will be powerful, memorable, formative, exciting, full of adventure and filled with incredible growth of your mind. There will also be sadness, social drama, peer pressure, confusion and perhaps heartbreak. Stay true to yourself, stay connected to your family and put effort into meaningful friendships that you value most. Good friends from your teenage years will be your friends for life!

You have the world in front of you and your family and friends behind you in every step of the way. Enjoy this adventure with no regrets!!!

With Love,
Ms. Melly

Dear Maya,

Turning 13 is so exciting. There are so many fun things, changes, and challenges you will be experiencing and all of it is great character building.

You have two wonderful parents to help guide you along the way. Hopefully, you'll take what you've learned at home and apply them to what you experience out on your own.

I have no doubt you'll make smart decisions.

Enjoy these next few chapters in your life and remember to be the creator of your own happiness!

Love,
Ms. Irene

You are the sky. Everything else is just the weather.
Pema Chodron
Buddhist Nun and Teacher, USA

Dear Maya,

From the moment I began thinking about inspirational life quotes, slips of paper began falling out from between books and off shelves. I was reminded that life has a way of answering our smallest request.

- **Have Faith!!** These 2 words could sum up a life's journey. *"What two words of wisdom would you give your younger self?"* I remember this questions from of all places my Facebook feed. Have faith was my immediate response. It reminded me that life is a journey filled with twists and turns and that it does not always go as planned. Your success can be summed up by the way you handled your life assignments.
- "The winds of God's Grace are always blowing, it is for us to raise the sails"
  ---Ramakrishna

This reminds me that by doing good, good will come by being open to it.

- Count your blessings because a grateful heart is a happy heart.
- I will love the light for it shows me the way, yet I will endure the darkness because it shows me the stars. ---Og Mandino
- Life is too short to wake up with regrets so love the people who treat you right. Forget about the ones who don't. Believe everything happens for a reason. If you get a second chance, grab it with both hands. If it changes your life, let it. Nobody promised life would be easy. They just promised it would be worth it. --Harvey McKay
- Life will let you get away with something for awhile, but sooner or later, you will pay the price. Everything you do in life causes the effects that you experience. When you get the bill, be prepared to pay. ----Iyanla Vanzant

- The following verses were written by Mother Teresa. They are great words to remind us how to live in joy and peace.
  - Do it anyway.
  - People are often unreasonable, irrational and self-centered. Forgive them anyway.
  - If you are kind, people may accuse you of selfish, ulterior motives. Be kind anyway.
  - If you are successful, you will win some unfaithful friends and some genuine enemies.
  - If you are honest and sincere people may deceive you. Be honest and sincere anyway.
  - What you spend years creating, others could destroy overnight. Create anyway.
  - If you find serenity and happiness, some maye be jealous. Be happy anyway.
  - The good you do today, will often be forgotten. Do good anyway.
  - Give the best you have and it will never be enough. Give your best anyway.
  - In the final analysis, it is between you and God. It was never between you and them anyway.

Love,
Ms. Madeline

Maya,

This year begin your journey into womanhood. Women are gentle, kind, thoughtful and strong. We give life and nurture all God's children. You are the choices you make. Know that what you cultivate now will become your memories and the stepping stones to your future. Friendships can last forever. Cherish them.

The world around you may seem to be moving so quickly, that can be exciting. And, there is no need to rush. Time and wisdom are on your side. You have a very special gift to share with the world. Allow yourself to find, grow and blossom into that purpose. Enjoy this time of discovery. Become the woman you revere, the woman your mother and grandmother are already so proud of.

Love,
Ms. Andrea

Your life is right now. It is not later. It's not in that time of retirement. It's not when the lover gets here. It's not when you move into the new house. It's not when you get the better job. Your life is right now. It will always be right now.
Esther Hicks/Abraham
Inspirational Speaker, USA

Oh My Dear Maya,

Your beauty makes me smile. I don't believe I've ever seen a picture without you smiling. We met many years ago as you attended a baby shower with your Mom. You were the only child there and yet, you sat very attentively. I thought then, she is a fairy. That inquisitive Bumble Bee that flies from tree to tree looking for something new to see.

As you move to your next stage of growth and development, you will encounter people who will not love the beauty that you see. But fly onto the next tree. The Universe is waiting for you to be exactly what you will come to be. Full of Joy, Peace and Light like a fairy shining in the night. Spread your wings and fly my child. For your beauty makes me smile.

With All My Love,
Ms. Brenda

Do small things with great love.
Mother Teresa
Christian Saint, India

Dear Maya,

Accept your body the way it is! Everyone is different. There is no perfect body type! Concentrate on staying active and being healthy and strong. If you do that, everything else will fall into place. It took me 40 years to realize and accept this!!

Always surround yourself with great girlfriends!! Make sure they are supportive and positive. Don't be afraid to let go of the negative ones. Boyfriends come and go, but a great friend can get you through anything!

When you are figuring out what you want to do in life, find something you are passionate about! Choose a career that helps to fuel that passion! Going to work everyday is much easier when you love what you do and feel that you are making a difference.

Enjoy being a teenager! These are going to be some of the best years of your life! This is the time when you start getting more independent and enjoy different freedoms!

Love,
Ms. Lisa

I have learned over the years that when one's mind is made up, this diminishes fear; knowing what must be done does away with fear.
Rosa Parks
Activist for Civil Rights, USA

Sweet, strong Maya,

I can't even begin to count the number of times I have looked over at your mom during a soccer game and said "I love watching Maya play!" It has been an absolute joy to watch you grow and change over the past several years. I remember the sweet little girl that seemed so timid and scared on the field and now.....NOW, you are a true force to be reckoned with. You are strong and fierce and tough and powerful! I love how you have grown into a player and a young lady who knows how to stand strong and not let anyone push you around.

My hope for you, and all of our soccer girls, is that you continue to grow as a player and as a person, and that you wear your confidence with pride.

Happy Birthday!

Love,
Ms. Willow

The highest form of wisdom is kindness.
Talmud
Judaism

Dearest Maya,

I have had the great privilege to get to know you and your family over the past several years and it has been remarkable watching you grow from a quiet, gentle little girl into a strong, mature young lady. I feel so blessed that you and your wonderful family are in my life.

I see so many similarities between you and Ava and how exciting it is that you will both be celebrating such an amazing milestone this year as you turn 13. It's hard to believe that we used to watch you two just starting out on the soccer field barely knowing the rules, to now transforming into such strong, talented players.

Becoming a woman is an exciting time and as I think back to my time as a teenager, I feel that I learned a few lessons that I would love to share with you:

- It is very important to surround yourself with good people and great friends. They will be a support system for you and your true friends will always celebrate with you and want the best for you. They will also build you up when you need strength. It's not about the quantity of friends; it's about the quality of friendships.
- Remember to appreciate each moment, as time certainly goes by fast. The older you get, the quicker it seems to move. Enjoy the quiet times, the big moments, and everything in between.
- Allow each moment, whether good or bad, happy or sad (and like everyone else, you will have your share of sad/bad times), a learning experience. This will help you to become a stronger person.
- Don't feel that beauty is defined by your looks. Confidence, kindness and strength make you beautiful. But a smile is always a plus!

- Never be afraid to be smart. It will pave the way for your future and lead to success. Knowledge is power! (I learned that from a 1980's Schoolhouse Rock video--ha!)
- And finally, appreciate your parents for all that they say and all that they do. You may not understand it now or during those times when you really do not want to listen to advice, but not until I went off to college did I truly understand why they had certain rules or were always interested in my personal life, where I went and who I was with. The advice that they will provide is heartfelt, although at times you may feel that it is prying or lecturing. But they just want the best for you and by being involved, it will help you lead your best life. Now being a mom myself, I am always so honored when people tell me how I am so much like my mom. It is such a compliment. You are so fortunate that you also have one amazing mother who will be such an amazing role model for you! She is a woman who is kind, sincere, confident, brilliant, generous and a great friend and you share all of those same fabulous qualities. Be proud of the girl you have been and the woman you are becoming!

Love,
Ms. Mary Ellen

Dear Maya,

Happy 13th birthday! It has been about nine years since our paths first crossed in a loving, peaceful, enthusiastic classroom community. You were an integral part of forming that community because you were one of two "older" children; the younger children looked up to you figuratively and literally.

My teenage years started off a bit rocky as I transitioned from a safe zone where I knew everyone and they knew me, to a much larger school where I needed to pull from my strengths and develop new adaptive techniques. Moving to a different part of my city gave me an opportunity to make new friends and try new activities. My old friends, who shared my core values, provided stability as I branched out and explored new ways of looking at the world.

High school was fun with active participation in my classes and everything related to school. For my junior year, I ran for secretary of my graduating class but was defeated. I was discouraged but continued to stay involved in the clubs and activities that interested me. For my senior year, I ran for treasurer of my graduating class and was successful. I have never enjoyed being in the spotlight so creating a campaign and making speeches was a stretch for me. I persevered because I felt I could make a difference in the governance of my class.

Maya, I think I was on the right track. Do the things you love, with the people you love, but be open to new experiences even if they are a stretch. You are fortunate to be surrounded by people who support you. Talk with them, share your thoughts and feelings.

When encountering difficulties, remember that how you feel is based on a thought and that thought can be changed. Look for the "silver lining". One's attitude is a small thing that makes a big difference.

Wishing you a joyous journey filled with love and light,

Ms. Pam

Dearest Maya,

In thinking back on my own life at age 13, and having lived and grown 34 years since, a few things stand out to me as meaningful nuggets that I hope, by sharing with you now, might help you on the journey ahead.

First….you are incredibly blessed with a mom who chooses to live and parent consciously, with love and compassion as her guide! That in itself is a huge gift that you may occasionally forget or take for granted, so I want to remind you each time you read this. My mother did the best she was personally capable of at the time, but she never touched me (other than to hit me), never hugged me or told me that she loved me. So when your mom disciplines you, know that she is doing so because she loves you more than life itself, and it's the best way she knows how to help you at that time.

Second…..nobody has it all figured out----especially teenagers. (smile) They can act in confusing, disturbing, even hurtful ways at times, leaving you wondering "Why?" My best advice: "Forgive them, for they know not what they do." We rarely have the full picture of what someone has been through or is going through in their life, or why they may act out in destructive ways. Give people the benefit of the doubt, but stay true to yourself and focus on what brings you joy! Avoid getting sucked into drama; trust that the people who are meant to accompany you on your journey will be revealed in good time and are worth waiting for!

Third…..be a lighthouse, not a carpet. When you are diligent in keeping the larger part of you focused on your own spirit, your inner light will draw people to you. Nurture the relationships that are mutually beneficial and let the others go. Be careful to avoid energy vampires; don't let people walk all over you because they mistake your kindness for weakness.

Fourth......comparison always leads to feeling bad. It's a super slippery slope and sometimes we don't even realize when we are on it! Whether we think we're better, or think we're worse than another, neither is ultimately the truth. We are woven from the same material---love and consciousness and ultimately, returning to the same state from whence we came. When we compare, we are looking at mile 2 to 3 in a 10K...While someone (or you) may excel at a particular skill at a particular moment in time, things can change very quickly, so what's the point? Ask yourself: What does it matter who's better at "X" in the end? What relevance does it have to the reason I am here? How does it serve me or anyone to compare? Instead, strive to do your personal best in everything you do and let that be enough.

Fifth.....when you come to a fork in the road (there will be many), and you're not sure which way to go, follow the breadcrumb trail of JOY. Don't overthink it---go in the direction that most lights you up and know that you can never get it wrong and you'll never get it done. Life is a journey of unfolding experiences, one after another. NO matter how bad things seem, this too shall pass. Tune inward and take the path that excites you most. Let JOY be the needle of your compass!

Sixth......YOU ARE ENOUGH. There is nothing you need to do or think or say or be to deserve God's love. You ARE love and you ARE God. We are all God, like droplets of water from the ocean of love and consciousness. Everyone is deserving, everyone is already whole and complete just by BE-ing; treat each other so.

Finally......Maya, remain eternally, enthusiastically curious! This path called life is rarely straight; it has twists, turns, detours and obstacles. If you expect them and approach each one with a sense of enchantment and wonder about what's around the bend or through the challenge, life will become a joyful journey of unexpected delight!

For your 13th birthday, and this beautiful coming of age into young womanhood...I wish for you to know that your spirit is equivalent to the light of thousands of outer suns, contained in a divinely designed vessel so that you may feel, see, hear, touch, taste, smell and experience LIFE! En-JOY every moment!!!

Abundant blessings,
Ms. Kelli

I raise up my voice, not so I can shout but so that those without a voice can be heard.
Malala Yousafzai
Activist, Pakistan

Dear Maya,

Happy 13th birthday! It is an honor to write some thoughts for you on this important occasion. In seven short teen years, you will become a young woman, possibly driving home from college for a visit, living with people you've yet to meet, maybe studying in another country.

Thinking about what to write to you led me to remember some of the women in my almost 63 years who showed me and are showing me how to be a woman.

The first word that came to mind was **to make**: actually two words, a gerund, a verb form. The women in my life were and are "makers." They did not need "maker spaces" as we say now. They never said, "Watch me, this will be important later." They just lived life. Without realizing it, I was absorbing the values that prompted the actions I saw.

So, who were/are these women and what did I learn from them? First what I learned....

I learned to make:

> Time
> Friends
> A reader
> A home
> An occasion to remember
> A confident woman
> A faith
> A career
> A character
> A life

How did they teach me? I'll tell you about them and you will see.

Agnes, "Mammy", my father's mother was the only grandmother I knew. She lived "far away" in Doylestown, PA. We did not see her often, but she wrote. She wrote to my parents and she wrote to me as soon as I could read. I read about her going to her quilting circle and bingo and shopping and how her cat left the gift of a mouse on her slippers for her to find in the morning. She wrote how grateful she was when I sent some of my school papers to show her how I was learning and told me how smart I must be to do so well. She wrote about what was growing in the garden and how she anticipated planting her vegetables and flowers. When we visited Mammy, she always just happened to have very large homemade cookies sitting in a metal tray on top of her refrigerator. Or she just happened to have two matching hand sewn quilts that just fit the new doll bunk beds I got for Christmas. Mammy had a way of telling a little girl "You are my youngest grandchild" as if that was a VIP status! Her letters always included how much she loved that youngest grandchild and she asked me to tell my parents to hug me for her.

Mary Clare, "Mom" lost her own mother years before I was born. She, her three sisters and six brothers remained fast friends all through life. One of Mom's favorite expressions was "You could make that" and she did. She made all of my clothes, doll clothes, curtains, knitted sweaters and vests, baby outfits for gifts, cakes for the carnival at church and flower arrangements for the May procession from the roses in her garden. She made a garden from plants given to her by my grandmother and her neighbors. Descendants of my grandmother's ferns live in my garden now.

Mom cooked. She made dinner everyday just about 360 days per year. The other days we were visiting someone or on a brief trip to Ocean City. Dinner was ready by 5:30 and it always included two vegetables, some kind of potato and any kind of meat my father would eat. She made candy Easter eggs and sugar Easter eggs with scenes inside and about 15 different kinds of Christmas cookies.

Mom listened. She listened to spelling words, prayers being learned, my piano lesson music, me banging out Christmas carols over and over and singing along, the sound of me typing high school papers late into the night while she was trying to sleep and complaints about everyone and everything. When I went to college, she listened to how much I thought I knew compared to her and how I thought she should do things such as exercise, get a job and become a feminist.

Mom went places---never far. She went: to mass every week, to the grocery store where each week I could select a Golden book or magazine from the kids' shelves in the front of the store, to the library and to help me get a card as soon as I could print my name, to school to be "room mother" and "milk money lady" and to buy a real Christmas tree for the first grade classroom, to Girl Scout trips and other and daughter "teas", to high school orchestra concerts where my clarinet squeaked, to watch my son's Halloween parades (he wore costumes that she made), to hear my son's piano recital, to sit on my brother's sofa with a granddaughter on each side and listen to them read Dr. Seuss books she bought for them, around the neighborhood to collect money for flowers anytime a neighbor died, to have coffee with her dear friend Mrs. Bert.

Mrs. Bert was Mom's best friend three houses away. Every day, they had coffee together in Bert's kitchen. It was easier that way because Bert had Sallie, who has Down's syndrome and occupied herself better at home. In 1953, when Sallie was born, the doctor said, "Put her in an institution" but Bert didn't listen. She took Sallie home and as she grew up, she played at our house and my mother and I went to all of her school events. Sallie and I are the same age.... almost. She was born in November and I was born the following March. Our moms were over 40 at the time. So...we visited Bert and pre-school me liked to sit under Bert's dining room table on "noodle days" while they talked in the kitchen. On noodle days, homemade noodles were drying on the dining room table, where a child under the table could reach up and grab one all the way around the edge, eating as she went. I do not remember Bert getting angry about that. I do remember getting butter toast, which I loved and I am told that one time I ate the side of a cake from that dining room table.

Aunt Rita was my godmother. Rita had two boys and always made them let me in the car first. "Ladies first," she would say. When my cousin Henry dropped his whole soda on her rug, she called to my uncle "Lou, Henry needs a new soda." When I dropped a whole lemon meringue in the middle of her living room during an after funeral lunch, she said, "She didn't mean it. The handle on the cake keeper broke." If you stopped at their house you got a snack or a meal. If it was Sunday, there were doughnuts. Her house was very tiny, a duplex with no room in the kitchen for a table, but many family events were held there. Aunt Rita "had room". As she was suffering her last illness in the hospital, she told me, "You're a good nurse," because I brushed her hair. At her funeral, the funeral home had to use all the rooms on the first floor because her "boys" came. Men in their 40s and 50s, who had "hung out" in her basement with its freezer full of an endless supply of frozen pizzas or who had been "her" cub scouts. All her favorite nieces and nephews came so that meant all of us.

Mrs. O and Mrs. E worked as librarians for Baltimore County when I was a "page", someone who worked shelving books. They were women who worked at a career, the first women I knew who did that (except for the sisters at school). They asked me what I was going to do after high school. Was I going to go to college? When I went to college, I would stop in to see them. They would ask "What are you studying?" Mrs. O told me about her college days and Mrs. E gave me materials she had used with her children when I began to work in a school. She was a mom and a librarian.....hmmmm.

Sister St. Joseph was my high school homeroom teacher. She noticed a girl who didn't seem able to make friends and she gave me a little scroll that said I was the "Susie Homemaker" of our classroom. She did not know that my home was one to which I could not bring friends. She **saw me** though. She saw someone who needed help, though she never knew the reason and at the time, I couldn't have told her. Sister showed us her potter's wheel in the convent and she made a ceramic medallion for each girl in the homeroom with a ribbon attached so we could wear it. It was a very "cool" thing to have in 1968. That medallion is in my jewelry box right now and the memory of someone who really SAW me will last. I plan to visit her soon.

Ms. L was the media specialist at Edgewood Elementary School library. It was my first job and I was her assistant, who at first, did not assist very well. One day she said, "When I ask you to do something, I want you to write it in this steno book and be sure to do it. I don't want to have to think about it anymore once I have told you, because I have my own work to do. I need to be able to count on you." She also said, "Make sure it is possible to do something before you tell students you will do it. Always keep your promises to them." Another time she mentioned that she always wore a jacket or vest at work along with a blouse (we say shirt now) because it looked more professional. She invited me to her house many times and I was in awe of the things she displayed from around the world and the way that she entertained so "easily." Her husband was a high level military officer and they had lived so many places while raising their two children. She managed to find a job as a teacher or school librarian everywhere they went. She used ideas and objects from her her travels to incorporate into her lessons. She opened my eyes to other cultures and world folktales.

Dr. R was my advisor at Catholic University when I was getting my Master's degree. She also taught children's literature and literature for young adults. She kept handing back my book reviews telling me to re-write, to realize that not everyone had the same frame of reference I had, that I had to explain, be clear, have an informed opinion. When she was satisfied, I felt wonderful. Dr. R offered to take me and others to visit former students in the schools where they worked. She always told them that I was "doing the job and doing it well although I did not have a Master's degree." At the time, I was working full time as an elementary media specialist. When my son was born, Dr. R said, "Of course I will make sure that you can come back to the Master's degree program even though you will need two semesters at home, not one as you said." She let me know that I could come back and that I WOULD finish.

Georgia T. and I met in 1979, my first assignment as a media specialist in charge of the library. Georgia was a classroom aide. She came to library class with her emotionally disturbed students who were in a special class at the school. They loved her and listened to her and I watched how she treated them. Georgia is a force of nature. She took me to my first "symphony showcase" house, to her mother's home in upstate New York near Canada, to Niagara Falls and to every event I never heard before! Seems she takes after her mom, who was about 85 when I visited. We came home after midnight and her mother got up from her bed and came bustling downstairs saying, "Let's have a snack so you girls can tell me all about your day." Georgia lived in Aberdeen, near the school and I lived 28 miles away. On nights when there were events at the school and I couldn't go home because it was too far away, she said, "Come to my house. Take a shower, eat, do whatever you want. If I'm not home, I'll just leave the door open." She did, too. She also threw a huge baby shower for me, listened to my worries after my divorce in 1994 and traveled back to Maryland from her retirement in New

York to be "maid of honor" at my second wedding in 2007. I can't wait to visit her again this spring.

Ann C. was my assistant in the library at Bel Air Middle School for ten years. She and I began working together the same year I became a single parent. When my birthday came around, there was always a card from the kids who were library helpers, cake and a celebration that morning before school. (Guess who made that happen?). Ann invited me to go for coffee after school. I always said, "No, I can't." She invited me to go shopping with her. I said, "No, I can't." She kept inviting me until one day I went for coffee......And it was fun and other people came and it seemed easier than I thought it would be to talk and laugh with them and we kept doing that. I began to call people and invite them to do things with me. If they said no, I called someone else and asked them another time. It seemed it was easier to make friends than I thought it would be.

So, Maya, these are a few women who've shown me the way in life. I could go on and list your mom and others at Freestate and more, but I think all this might have been too much. My hope for you is that you will notice those along the way who model how to live a good and fulfilling life. There are so many people to admire in this world. Most of those people are nearby all along the way. Treasure them. Learn from them. Love them and you will be blessed with good friends to accompany you through life.

Love and blessings,
Ms. Cathy

Dear Maya,

Finding joy and happiness amidst a sea of life stress is a woman's greatest strength!!

Love,
Ms. Anya

Prophecy states that it will be the women who walk with the power. We have an incredible journey and responsibility as women. All of our life, we are caretakers, walking with the Mother. We carry this within our being. For women to have the freedom in the heart to be able to express ourselves spiritually is very, very important. We must learn to stay balanced in the moment and give each moment 100 percent of our prayer. When we go off balance and get rocked by life, we need to bring ourselves back quickly to the moment, one moment at a time. Grandmother Flordemayo, Central America/New Mexico *Grandmothers Counsel the World*

Dear Maya,

This gift comes to you from your Auntie Karen. It is framed as an apology. My very first encounter with you was at my home on North Pulaski Street in West Baltimore. I offer this apology to you because in the moment that I met you, I felt that my best was not good enough.

I want you to understand that wherever you may find yourself in life, that your best is always good enough Maya. Let nobody tell you otherwise. Let not even you tell you otherwise. If you just remember to show up as your beautiful whole self, there is nothing more you can ask of yourself or give to anyone else.

This treasure I give to you.

God bless you sweetie,
Auntie Karen

Who acts from love is greater than who acts from fear.
Talmud
Judaism

Dear Maya,

Trust yourself; you are smarter and stronger than you believe.

When faced with a problem or a challenge, be quiet, be still. The answers are inside of you.

Love,
Ms. Erin

Our present sufferings cannot even be compared
to the glory that will be revealed to us
Romans 8:18 New English Translation Bible
Christianity

Just a few thoughts dear Maya…..

As you discover who you are and look toward your friends more, know that no one understands and loves you like your family.

Being authentic and true to who you are, above all else, is so liberating!!! Trends can be soooooo boring!!

Asking for help when you need it is not a sign of weakness, but is truly an indicator of strength.

XOXOXO,
Ms. Kia

There came a time when the risk to remain tight in the bud was more painful than the risk it took to blossom.
Anais Nin
Essayist, USA

Dear Maya,

Don't change so people will like you.

Be yourself and the right people will love the real you.

Be confident and wise.

Wish you all the best,
Ms. Humera

To truly love, it is necessary to drop the past and say, 'I start over, right here and right now, being a new me.'
Sai Maa, Guru/Spiritual Master, India
<u>Grandmothers Counsel the World</u>

Dear Maya,

Hello! I understand you are turning 13; what an incredible age you are about to enter!

My name is Gaye and I am very happy to say that I work with your amazing mom. I have raised two fantastic daughters; Jenna is 31 and Sam is 29, so needless to say, I am (a) pretty old and, (b) I have tons of experience with people your age. :) And because of my age, I can honestly say that I have seen and done a lot and can hopefully impart some sort of wisdom on those younger than me. So here goes...

I was born wayyyyyyy back in 1958, which was a very different time from today. When I was 5 years old, John F. Kennedy was assassinated, Martin Luther King Jr. gave his famous "I Have A Dream" speech, our phone was attached to the wall in our kitchen, and the TV's in my house all broadcast in black and white only. I lived through the Civil Rights Movement, the Vietnam War, the emergence of the Beatles and the rest of the British invasion, the moon landing, and so many other historical things, (remember I told you I am old). My aunt, who I thought was the coolest person on Earth, would take in strangers from all over the country who would come to DC where I grew up to participate in protests and marches. I used to love seeing all the picket signs in her yard. It's these kind of things that make huge impressions on young people.

When I was young, during the late 1960s, women's rights became a large social issue......not that it hadn't been in the past; women's rights go back to the days of Sojourner Truth and even further back than that. But in the 1960's inequality amongst races and genders were in the forefront of the social movement. Up to this point, most women took on the role of the stay-at-home-mom, taking care of her family and her house. Don't get me wrong; being a mom is THE GREATEST job in the world, but in those days, a woman didn't have many career choices. Support roles in offices offered women a glimpse into the corporate world, but there were very few opportunities for any sort of advancement. If a woman worked in the healthcare field, more than likely it was as a nurse and if a female worked in a factory, it was to "hold down the fort" until men returned from the war to take their jobs back, and then it was back home for most women. To say that women were considered second class citizens is an understatement. But with the 60s came an awakening led by strong women who decided the time had come to be equal to their male counterparts. It continues to be a struggle today and although so many strides have been made in the path to equality, we still have work to do. And the torch is about to be passed down to your generation of young women. Perhaps through your efforts, we will see a female president in this country, equal pay for equal work, and women's health issues become as important as those issues facing men. Don't be afraid to make your voice heard, not only for the continued struggle for women's rights, but for human rights throughout the world.

Let me end with this, in the culture in which I was raised, (unbeknownst to me when I was your age) it is a tradition for a girl to be slapped across the face when she enters womanhood, usually around the age of 13. It's symbolic of the pain that comes with being a woman, as well as the jolt of leaving childhood behind. My mother didn't warn me about this; I came bounding into her room one morning, proclaiming I had finally become a woman, and she slapped me. This was the first and only time I had been hit by either of my parents; I was shocked and I think my mom kind of enjoyed it! Years later, I warned my daughters of the tradition prior to gently tapping them on the cheek when they too became women. And I told them both this: being a woman is an honor; embrace all of the aspects of this. Don't let your teenage peers, as well as your peers at any age, influence you to the point where you lose yourself. Be proud of your intelligence and your compassion. Always think of others and how they may be in need of your help. Even though you may not believe it now, your mom is going to be right the majority of the time, regardless of how ridiculous that might sound to you. And, most importantly, be proud of yourself, stay strong in your convictions, and always believe in you. Don't be afraid to grow, experience and spread your wings in this wonderful life of ours.

Welcome to womanhood. Happy birthday!!

Love,
Ms. Gaye

With every difficulty, there is relief.
Qur'an 94:5
Islam

Dear Maya,

Always live your very best life. Pursue true happiness with wild abandon.

Here is the rub: a person can only find TRUE happiness through both CHALLENGING AND CARING FOR THEMSELVES physically, intellectually, emotionally and spiritually AND by being in the service of others.

As human beings truly learn by watching what others do, it is not a selfish thing to live the life of your dreams. Let others see you pursue true happiness and receive the gift of learning how to do the same.

Ms. Jen

The secret to living well and longer is: eat half, walk double, laugh triple and love without measure.
Tibetan Proverb
Buddhism

Maya,

Love yourself
Respect yourself
Be honest with yourself
Forgive yourself
Nurture yourself
Educate yourself
Accept yourself

We love you Maya! Happy birthday!

Love,
Ms. Patricia

*One life is all we have and we live it as we believe
in living it. But to sacrifice what you are and to live
without belief that is a fate more terrible than dying.*
Joan of Arc
Christian Saint, France

Dear Maya,

I am so grateful that you are in Ada's life. I see you as a kind, gentle friend with good roots to grow well.

I pray that you continue to grow in character, honor and laughter.

Happy 13th year!!

Love,
Mrs. Jamie

We have all known the long loneliness and
we have learned that the only solution is love
and that love comes from community.
Dorothy Day
Social Worker/Pacifist, USA

My dearest Maya,

There are very few things I truly know. But one of the things I know is that there are many beautiful people and places on this earth.

The second thing that I know is that we all have one best friend who is with us always. And that best friend is with us through all of the most brilliant celebrations and joys in life. That same best friend is with us as well in our deepest sorrows. That best friend is our soul.

So my advice to you is to enjoy every day seeking always the beauty in each interaction with people and with the environment.

My second piece of advice to you is to cultivate your relationship with your best friend, with your soul. Many people do many things to cultivate that relationship. My suggestion is to always find your personal way to be in relationship with your soul.

I will share with you that each morning when I wake up I feel my heart and connect with my soul, my best friend. I feel gratitude for my soul and for the new day. At night I also connect and notice my heart and soul. I feel gratitude for all the many interactions and blessings I've had that day and thank my soul for her constant companionship and guidance.

Of course I also check in with my soul throughout the day (when I remember or am in need of help!) Sometimes I sit still like in meditation, or go for a quiet walk, paint, journal or pet my cat. Those activities also help me to connect.

My wish for you is that you have great adventures every day of your life. I also wish for you to have a most glorious relationship with the most important person in your life, YOU!!

I see you as a Smart, Creative, Gorgeous and Courageous young woman. I see you as having many of the qualities of a Wonderful Woman.

Even though I might not get to see you often, it has been an honor and a privilege to watch you grow.

With love,
Ms. Betsey

Dear Maya,

Congratulations on becoming a teen! Adolescence is the most beautiful time in life. It looks like a morning fog, hazy and subtle, but suitable for wandering.

Think big, dream big, try all of your potentials since you have enough time to fulfill them. Have wide interests and do not give yourself limitations. Follow your heart and focus, dig deep.

Make good friends and care about other people. Kindness will make you go far, and I am sure that is your strength.

The last thing I want to share with you is that I believe grit is the key to success. And I know that's what your heart is made of.

Best wishes for a colorful and memorable youth!

Ms. Mali

Whenever you are creating beauty around
you, you are restoring your own soul.
Alice Walker
Novelist/Activist, USA

Maya,

When I first set about in planning this book for you, I knew that it would be special. Coincidentally, or not by any coincidence at all (which is how the universe works), this outpouring of love has been healing for my 13 year old self. This book truly has been a gift for me too and I thank you for inspiring me to create it.

As I write this letter to you, I am also writing this letter to myself--- to acknowledge and heal that teenage part of me who felt incredibly lonely. I know that in showing up to support myself, I am more fully able to support you, your sister and everyone else in my life. It is first an inside job. So here goes...

Maya, I recognize your beautiful, sensitive, honest soul who cares so deeply about her family and friends because that is something we have in common. I now know that my sensitivity and deep love for others is a gift to both me and the world, but back then I didn't understand. My parent's separation and divorce and many of the details that came before, during and after it were very painful and during much of my teenage years, my life seemed out of control. I did not know what the future (or even each day) would hold and I struggled to find security and a safe place to simply be seen. I went through my school days hardly speaking, to anyone. Most of my high school friends moved on as I continued to withdraw and I began to feel more and more unseen. In grasping for control, I was afraid to "rock the boat" with my needs and desires so I kept them hidden and played my self-chosen role of responsible student and daughter very well. Looking back now, I see that I there were people in my life who would have helped me if I only would have asked.

During this time, I journaled and wrote poetry alot. It was a way I could express myself if only to an audience of one. I believe this was one of the things that saved me---having an avenue to let my feelings out. I still have this as a practice to this day. In addition to writing, I found another lifeline. It came in the form of my church's youth group. As I sat in our church service each week, I saw youth group events in the church bulletin. One day I decided to stretch myself and attend an event. And then attended another and then another. I started to make friends and be noticed there. I joined the youth group volleyball team and later I was asked to join the youth group leadership team. I loved having a place to go and I began to slowly let my guard down so I could connect with the others.

I also began to feel a stronger connection to a power greater than myself. Even though I didn't fully agree with all the church's doctrine, I felt a peaceful energy when I was at church, singing the hymns and participating in the ceremony of the mass. I enjoyed being a part of a community and knowing that I was not alone. Even now, many years later and having no specific religious affiliation, I am in awe and feel peace whenever I walk into a house of worship. It is one avenue for direct connection to God and in those years of my life, I was grateful to have this connection.

Between my junior and senior years of high school, I went away to a camp out of state. There, I began to experience myself and others in new ways and I realized that I could change my "story". When I got home from camp, I told my parents that I wanted to go to a new school and have a new start, even if it was only for my senior year. Gratefully, they heard me and made the switch. In my new school, I began to open myself up to new opportunities and new friends. I was still more of a listener than a speaker, but I was learning little by little to trust myself and others.

The following year, I chose a large college where I could experience many different things and embraced all that I was learning about myself. I joined an outdoor recreation club in which I eventually became the president and won an award for outstanding leadership. I started working at a dining hall on campus and eventually became a student manager. I even tried out for an acapella singing group and though I didn't make it, I loved taking the risk. I also applied for and did not get accepted into a graduate program at my college and even though I was disappointed in the beginning, the door that closed then opened up the door to meeting your dad. We can both be grateful for that!

As the years continue to tick by, I am learning to listen with intent for that voice inside of myself that knows the best for me---not the role that I created to protect my sensitive self when I was younger, but the real me---my soul's deepest calling. I am realizing that when I get quiet, when I tune out all the demands of life, I connect to my own divinity. These days, spending quiet time in nature is when I am most connected.

I am learning that my power comes from stating what I want and what I feel and what I believe no matter what, being courageous even when others may not agree. I am also learning that allowing myself to be vulnerable, asking for help and taking risks allows me to connect more with others and with my true desires. The more I practice, the more I feel good inside and the more I radiate that positive feeling outward. I then see this love reflected back to me by the people in my life. They know how to treat me because I know how to treat myself.

It has taken me many years to truly feel confidence in myself (well, maybe not in my cooking skills!). And I am still learning more each day. What I do know for certain now is that being true to my inner voice and choosing joy and gratitude in the moment is the only way I want to live.

And this is my wish for you too, sweetheart. That you nurture your soul's calling and stand tall in courage, joy and gratitude in order to make all your wishes come true. This life is a wonderful adventure.

All experiences are learning opportunities. There is no "perfect", no "right way", no "have to's" and no "should be's". It is all possible and you, my love, are infinitely creative.

You Maya, and you my dear reader, are supported. You have a community of women around you--holding space for you to be all you desire. Women who know how to laugh and have fun. Women who know how to cry and feel pain. Women who know how to listen deeply and how to speak their thoughts.

As we rise up in our divine femininity, let us embrace the men in our lives. Let us recognize that they are a part of the oneness too as are all the living beings on this Earth. As conflict arises, let us remember that we are all mirrors for each other, reflecting back what is rising up in us. Choose loving boundaries. Choose gratitude. Choose authenticity. Choose lightness and fun. Choose YOUR joy.

Maya, I am grateful beyond words that you chose me to be your mother. You made my dream of being a mom first come true and have brought so much Maya Joy into my life! I look forward to many, many more memories together on our journey this time around.

With all my love,
Mom

Love recognizes no barriers. It jumps hurdles, leaps fences, penetrates walls to arrive at its destination full of hope.
Maya Angelou
Writer/Activist, USA

Acknowledgments

I have heartfelt gratitude for all the women who so bravely shared their stories and their wisdom in this book. Thank you for being a part of my village. Thank you also to the women who sent their stories in thought----those who are currently on this Earth and those who have left this Earthly plane. Our collective voices are compelling and fearless and are creating a path of healing for our world.

I honor the moms in my life, specifically my mother, my step-mother and my mother-in-law. Thank you for your expression of love. I also honor the souls of my two namesake grandmothers: one, Regina O'Sullivan, who I never met in this lifetime and yet still feel often in spirit. And the other, Mary Karl, who I spent lots of happy memories with and who I promised, moments before her passing, that I would take care of her great-granddaughters and work to heal our family's lineage.

Maya--thank you for being my muse. Thank you for inspiring me to reconnect with my 13 year old self and open my passionate voice to a wider audience. You are a strong and powerful force!

Brooke--thank you for modeling the lightness of being and reminding me everyday that life is meant to be fun. Looking forward to the creation of your book next year as you turn 13!

Tony--thank you for holding the space for me to explore my passions and purpose. Your love is a gift to me and I am eternally grateful for all of our adventures!

About the Author

For over 25 years, Gina Andreone Strauss has worked as a teacher and advisor in a variety of educational settings. Her advanced degrees in counseling and healing arts add a unique dimension to her teaching style and interactions with students and their families. She is an advocate for conscious parenting and is mindful of how our children serve as mirrors to us. Gina believes that much can be learned from life's experiences and recognizes the wealth of positive thought that can be gleaned from small day-to-day moments. She lives in Baltimore with her husband, two daughters and a herd of cats.

Printed in the United States
By Bookmasters